KINDER KOLLEGE

Primary Bible Lessons

L. M. Logan
Patrice Juah
Ophelia S. Lewis

Village Tales Publishing
MINNEAPOLIS, MN

Copyright © 2020 by Liberia Literary Society
All rights reserved. No part of this publication may be reproduced, distributed or transmitted in any form or by any means, without prior written permission.

www.liberialiterarysociety.org

Village Tales Publishing
www.villagetalespublishing.com
www.oass.villagetalespublishing.com
www.villagetalespublishing.com/childrensbooks

Book Cover by OASS
ISBN-13: 9781945408564
LCCN 2020904396

A Liberia Literary Society
Educational Project

Printed in the USA

This book belongs to:

_____

How to care for your book.

1. Read with clean hands.

2. Turn pages carefully.

3. Keep your book in your bookbag when you're not reading it.

4. Keep your book close to you when reading, so that you don't drop it.

5. Use a bookmark to save your page in a book.

6. Keep your book away from food and drinks.

7. Only draw, write, and color where instructed to.

8. Keep your book away from younger siblings and pets.

Contents

The Bible 5
The Old Testament 5
The New Testament 6
The Creation 7
God Made Me 9
God's Family 10
The Golden Rule 11
Baby Jesus 13
Jesus Calms the Storm 16
Jesus Feeds the Crowd 18
Who Touched Me? 20
Jesus Raises a Dead Girl 21
The Easter Story 22
'Psalm 23' 24
How to Pray 25
The Lord's Prayer 26
When I'm Afraid 28
Fruit of the Spirit 29
God's Laws for us. 32
Moses 33
52 Bible Verses to Memorize 34
Daniel 38
Joseph and His Colorful Coat 40
Noah Builds the Ark 42
Jonah and the Big Fish 44
David and Goliath 46
Job 48
True or False 50
Birth of Jesus 51
The Easter Story Domino Difference 52
Plenty of Fish 53
Joseph's Coat of Many Colors 54
Answers 55
What Makes Me Special 56

The Bible

The Bible is God's Word. It is a very important book. It tells the truth about God and His world. It is full of stories and they are all true - not fiction.

Even though the Bible is very old, it is still important today. The Bible shows us how to live a good life. It is full of advice, stories, poetry, and so much more. There are stories about evil kings, angels with powers, fire from the sky, and most important, the story about a little baby named, Jesus.

The Bible has 66 books, 39 in the Old Testament and 27 in the New Testament.

The Old Testament

Genesis	2 Chronicles	Daniel
Exodus	Ezra	Hosea
Leviticus	Nehemiah	Joel
Numbers	Esther	Amos
Deuteronomy	Job	Obadiah
Joshua	Psalms	Jonah
Judges	Proverbs	Micah
Ruth	Ecclesiastes	Nahum
1 Samuel	Song of Solomon	Habakkuk
2 Samuel	Isaiah	Zephaniah
1 Kings	Jeremiah	Haggai
2 Kings	Lamentations	Zechariah
1 Chronicles	Ezekiel	Malachi

The New Testament

Matthew
Mark
Luke
John
Acts
Romans
1 Corinthians
2 Corinthians
Galatians
Ephesians
Philippians
Colossians
1 Thessalonians
2 Thessalonians
1 Timothy
2 Timothy

Titus
Philemon
Hebrews
James
1 Peter
2 Peter
1 John
2 John
3 John
Jude
Revelation

The Creation

God made everything.

God is Awesome!

Verse to Memorize
In the beginning,
God created the heavens
and the earth.
Genesis 1:1

DAY 1
God made light and darkness.

DAY 2
God made water and sky.

DAY 3
God made land and plants.

DAY 4
God made the sun, moon, and stars.

DAY 5
God made birds and sea animals.

DAY 6
God made land animals and people.

DAY 7
God rested from his work.

God Made Me
I am special.

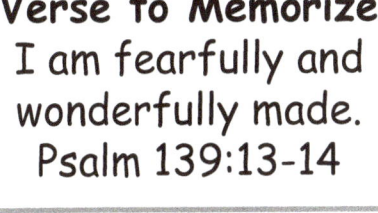

Verse to Memorize
I am fearfully and wonderfully made.
Psalm 139:13-14

God made me from my head to my toes.

He gave me two eyes and one little nose.

God made me extra special, There is no one like me!

He made me part of His own family!

Verse to Memorize
For those who are led by the Spirit of God are the children of God.
Romans 8:14

God's Family

We are part of God's Family.

God gave us two families. Our families have mothers and fathers, brothers, sisters, dogs and cats. God's family is led by Him. We are all God's children.

God gave me a family at home.

God gave me a family at church.

The Golden Rule

How do I want to be treated?

> **Verse to Memorize**
> Do to others
> what you would have
> them do to you.
> Matthew 7:12

When a friend is hurting,
Don't just watch them cry. Help
them to feel better, give it a try!

When it's time to play,
Be gentle and be kind,
Share toys and take turns.
Don't leave a friend behind.

When a friend needs help,
Think of what to do.
Be a friend and help them,
They'd do the same for you!

So... how will I treat others?

Do to others
what you would
have them do to you.

| Good friend do's |

Get along. Help.

| Good friend don'ts |

Don't lie. Don't laugh at others.

Baby Jesus

Long ago, God sent the angel Gabriel to a young woman named Mary. He told her, "You will have a son; name Him, Jesus.

Mary was confused; she was not yet married to Joseph. The angel said, "The Holy Spirit will do a miracle, because your baby is the Son of God."

Then the angel told Joseph the same thing in a dream. Joseph was to help Mary look after Jesus.

Joseph trusted and obeyed God. He also obeyed his country's laws. Because of a new law, he and Mary had to go to their hometown, Bethlehem, to pay their taxes.

It took them a long time to get there because they rode on a donkey.

Mary was ready to have her baby. But Joseph could not find a room anywhere. All the hotels were full.

Finally, someone felt bad for them and offered them a place to stay, a small barn where animals were kept.

Mary and Joseph were thankful. It was warm, and there was plenty of straw to lay on. That night an exciting thing happened: Mary and Joseph had a baby! But this wasn't just any baby, he was Baby Jesus! The one who would save the world.

Nearby, shepherds guarded their sleeping flocks. God's angel appeared and told them the wonderful news.

"There is born to you this day in the city of David a Savior, who is Christ the Lord. You will find the Baby lying in a manger."

Forty days later, Joseph and Mary brought Jesus to the temple in Jerusalem. There a man named Simeon praised God for the Baby, while old Anna, another servant of the Lord, gave thanks.

Sometime later, a special star led 3 Wise Men from an Eastern country to Jerusalem. "Where is He who is born King of the Jews?" they asked. "We want to worship Him."

The star led the Wise Men to the exact house where Mary and Joseph lived with the young child. Kneeling in worship, the travelers gave Jesus rich gifts of gold and perfume.

Christmas Day celebrates the birth of Jesus Christ.

Jesus Calms the Storm

One evening, Jesus said to his disciples, "Let's cross to the other side."

The disciples got into a boat with Jesus to row across the Sea of Galilee.

Soon, it looked like a storm was coming up.

A big storm came up.

Waves beat into the boat. It was about to be swamped.

The disciples were afraid.

But Jesus was alsleep in the stern of the boat.

They woke Jesus. "Teacher, don't you care that we are all about to drown?"

Jesus woke up. He said to them, "You are afraid because you do not have faith." Then, he looked toward the clouds.

Jesus said, "Peace! Be still."

The wind stopped. There was calm on the water.

Jesus Feeds the Crowd

Many people followed Jesus everywhere he went. One day when he came to the beach, he saw a huge crowd waiting for him.

Jesus took care of them all day. He prayed with some. He made those who were sick, well. He told them about God's love.

The disciples said to Jesus, "It is late, send them home to eat. "They don't need to leave," Jesus said. "You give them food."

"All we have is five loaves of bread and two fish," the disciples said.

Jesus took the five loaves of bread and two fish in his hand. He lifted the basket up to heaven and blessed it.

"Here," he said to the disciples. "Feed the people."

Everybody ate until they were full.

The disciples filled twelve baskets with leftovers.

Who Touched Me?

Everywhere Jesus went with his disciples, a big crowd followed him.

One day, in the crowd was a woman who had been bleeding for twelve years. She had spent all her money on doctors. They did not help her. In fact, she grew worst.

She said to herself, "If I touch his clothes, I will be healed."

She touched his clothes. Instantly, her bleeding stopped.

Jesus said to her, "Your faith has made you well."

Jesus Raises a Dead Girl

"My little daughter is about to die," Jairus said to Jesus. "Please, come and touch her."

But the people said to Jairus, "Don't bother Jesus. Your daughter is dead."

"Don't be sad, Jairus," Jesus said. "Only believe." Then Jesus went to Jairus' house. The people were crying.

Jesus said, "Why are you crying? She is not dead. She is sleeping."

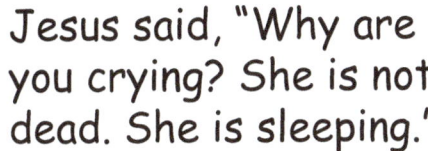

Jesus took the little girl's hand. He said, "little girl, get up!"

The little girl got up and walked around.

Jairus was happy again. He hugged his little daughter.

Jesus said, "Give her something to eat."

The Easter Story

After dinner, Jesus went to the garden to pray. He knew something was going to happen. Some men came and took Jesus away. They dressed him in a purple robe and put a crown of thorns on his head. Then, Jesus carried the cross up the hill. He died on the cross. Darkness came over all of the earth.

When Jesus died his friends were sad. They put him in a tomb. A large stone was place in front of the tomb. Soldiers stood nearby to see that no one rolled the stone away.

 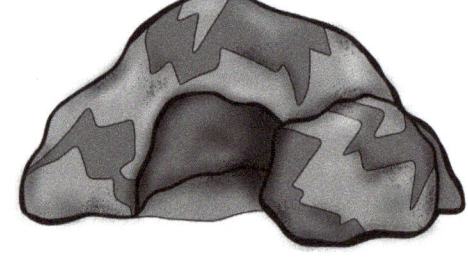

 For 3 days Jesus' body lay in the tomb. Then in the morning of the third day, an angel came and rolled the stone away. When the soldiers saw the angel, they were afraid.

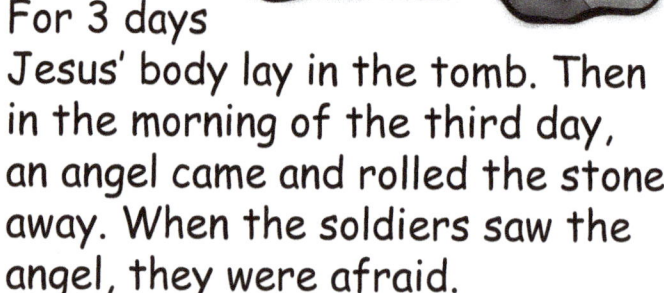 

The next morning, Mary and some other women came to the tomb. They saw that the stone had been rolled away. It was empty!

"Where is Jesus?" they asked. An angel appeared and said, "He is Risen!"

Jesus died so that we can all live again after we die. We have Easter to remind everyone of the day Jesus arose from the dead.

Before Jesus went back to heaven, He told his disciples to tell everyone the good news. Anyone who believes in Jesus as their Savior can live with Him forever in heaven. Jesus died for our sins. But He didn't stay dead. He rose again from the dead on the third day. And that is the wonderful story of Easter!

Psalm 23

The Lord is my shepherd,
I shall not want;
He makes me lie down in green pastures.
He leads me beside still waters;
He restores my soul.
He leads me in paths of righteousness
for His name's sake.

Even though I walk through the valley
of the shadow of death,
I fear no evil;
for You are with me;
Your rod and Your staff,
they comfort me.

Surely goodness and mercy
shall follow me all the days of my life;
And I shall dwell in the house
of the Lord forever.

How to Pray

PRAISE (thumb) – Praise is telling God how great He is and talking about all the great things that God has done.

THANKS (1st finger) – Thanking God for the things He has done and the things He has given us.

SORRY (middle finger) – Telling God the things we've done that we know He wouldn't want us to do. Tell Him we're sorry and ask Him to forgive us.

ASK (ring finger) – Asking God for the things that we need. This is the time to ask for things we need, not just things we want.

OTHERS (pinky) – We pray for others and it means asking God to help other people. We can pray for our family, our friends, people in our church and other people who need to hear about Jesus.

The Lord's Prayer

Give us this day our daily bread.

Forgive us our sins as we forgive others. . .

 Lead us not into temptation...

 Deliver us from evil...

Thine is the kingdom, and the power and glory, forever! Amen.

When I'm Afraid

When I'm afraid, like Daniel was in the lion's den,
I will trust God to protect me.

Verse to Memorize
When I am afraid, I put my trust in You.
Psalm 56:3

I will say my prayers befor I go to bed. I will put my trust in God!

When I am alone,
I will put my trust in God!

When lightning flashes,
I will put my trust in God!

When dogs bark loudly,
I will put my trust in God!

When it is dark,
and I feel scared,
I will put my trust in God!

Fruit of the Spirit

I let the Holy Spirit produce fruit in my life.

Galatians 5:22-23

Love means to like very much. We should love each other.

It is good to be happy when someone else wins or receives something. Would you want others to be happy for you?

Getting along with others.

Staying calm when dealing with something that is hard, but needs to get done.

Show kindness.

Sometimes we need to think of other people before thinking of ourselves.

Always be a friend when someone is sad.

When we use our manners, we are being gentle toward others. We hold doors for people, help them pick something up that they might have dropped, wait our turn in line, and use inside voice when in the building.

We have control over our actions by standing in line nicely while waiting for everyone to line up.

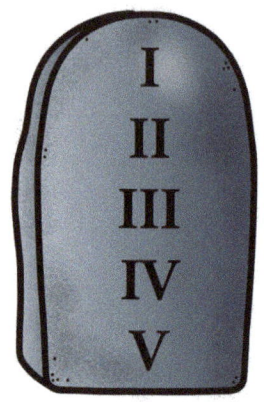 # The TEN COMMANDMENTS

God's Laws for us.

 **1** Love God more than you love anything else.

 **2**  Don't make anything in your life more important than God.

 **3** Always say God's name with love and respect.

 **4**  Honor the Lord by resting on the sabbath day.

Moses

 Love and respect your mother and father.

 Never hurt anyone.

  Always be faithful to your husband or wife.

 Don't take anything that isn't yours.

 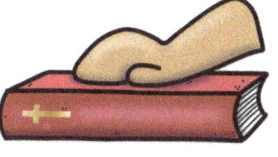 Always tell the truth.

 Be happy for what you have. Don't wish for other people's things.

52 Bible Verses to Memorize

Acts 16:31 Believe in the Lord Jesus Christ, and you will be saved.	1 John 4:19 We love because he first loved us.	Proverbs 14:5 A honest witness does not lie, a false witness breaths lies.
Matthew 22:39 You shall love your neighbor as yourself.	Psalm 145:9 The LORD is good to all.	Genesis 16:13 You are the God who sees.
Philippians 4:4 Rejoice in the Lord always. I will say it again: Rejoice!	Numbers 6:24 The Lord bless you and keep you.	Colossians 3:2 Set your minds on things above, not on earthly things.
Ephesians 4:30 And do not grieve the Holy Spirit.	Colossians 3:16 Let the word of Christ dwell in you richly.	1 John 5:3 This is love for God: to obey his commands.
Romans 10:13 Everyone who calls on the name of the Lord will be saved.	Proverbs 3:5 Trust in the Lord with all your heart.	Hebrews 13:8 Jesus Christ is the same yesterday, today and forever.
Psalm 150:6 Let everything that has breath praise the Lord.	Romans 3:23 All people have sinned and come short of the glory of God.	Matthew 5:14 You are the light of the world.

52 Bible Verses to Memorize

Psalm 145:9 The Lord is good to all.	Colossians 3:20 Children, obey your parents in all things.	James 1:17 Every good gift and every perfect gift is from above.
Matthew 28:20 I am with you always.	1 John 3:23 Love one another.	Psalm 56:3 "When I am afraid, I put my trust in You.
Ephesians 4:32 Be kind to one another.	Psalm 119:105 Your word is a lamp to my feet and a light for my path.	Psalm 118:24 This is the day the Lord has made; Let us rejoice and be glad in it.
Psalm 136:1 Give thanks to the Lord, for he is good. His love endures forever.	Luke 6:31 Do to others as you would have them do to you.	Philippians 4:13 "I can do all things through Christ who gives me strength."
Psalm 138:1 I will praise thee with my whole heart.	John 10:11 I am the good shepherd.	Matthew 6:24 No one can serve two masters.
Proverbs 30:5 Every word of God proves true.	Ephesians 6:1 Children, obey your parents in the Lord, for this is right.	John 11:35 Jesus wept.

52 Bible Verses to Memorize

Deuteronomy 6:5 You shall love the LORD your God with all your heart and with all your soul and with all your might.	**Corinthians 10:31** Whatever you do, do everything for the glory of God.	**Psalm 19:1** The heavens declare the glory of God.
Genesis 1:1 In the beginning, God created the heavens and the earth.	**Psalm 139:14** I praise you God, for I am fearfully and wonderfully made.	**Isaiah 43:5** Do not be afraid for I am with you.
Ecclesiastes 12:13 Fear God and keep his commandments.	**Matthew 28:6** He is not here, he is risen!	**Acts 5:29** We must obey God rather than men.
1 Thessalonians 5:17 Pray without ceasing.	**Isaiah 26:4** Trust in the Lord forever, for the Lord God is an everlasting rock.	**Psalm 46:10** Be still, and know that I am God.
Proverbs 2:6 The Lord gives wisdom.	**Psalm 1:6** The LORD knows the way of the righteous, but the way of the wicked will perish.	**Psalm 150:6** Let everything that has breath praise the LORD!

52 Bible Verses to Memorize		
Galatians 6:7 Do not be deceived: God is not mocked, for whatever one sows, that will he also reap.		

Daniel

Daniel was a good man. He loved God. He always prayed to God. He also obeyed God.

He and his friends Shadrach, Meshach, and Abednego refused the king's food when they were just teenagers. They ate only vegetables. The king was not mad because they were honest and hard-working.

As Daniel grew older, he had many important jobs. He was a hard worker. King Darius, the new king, also liked Daniel. This made some men jealous.

The men made King Darius believe things about Daniel that were not true. King Darius ordered them to throw Daniel into a den full of hungry lions. So Daniel spent a whole night in that den.

But God sent an angel to protect Daniel. The angel shut the lions' mouths. Daniel was not harmed by the lions. God was faithful to protect Daniel who had put God first in his life.

Verse to Memorize
When I am afraid, I put my trust in You.
Psalm 56:3

Joseph and His Colorful Coat

Joseph was one of the youngest kids in his family. He had 9 older brothers, 1 older sister, and 1 younger brother. His father loved him very much. One day his dad gave him a beautiful coat. Joseph loved his new coat of many colors that his father made for him.

This coat was made of lots of different colors. Joseph showed his brothers his new coat. Joseph's brothers were angry with Joseph and jealous of his new coat. They were really jealous.

They were mean to him. They threw him into a well, which is a big hole in the ground usually filled with water. Joseph was scared.

Verse to Memorize
You intended to harm me, but God intended it for good...
Genesis 50:20

Instead of hurting Joseph, they decided to send him far away from home. As a large group of people were passing by they sold Joseph to them. He was taken from his family and his home to a land far away.

Joseph finally arrived in his new home. His new home was Egypt. He got a new job. He had to take care of a man named Potipher's house. Potipher was really rich. Joseph was in charge of everything.

One day Potipher's wife wanted Joseph to do something wrong. Joseph said no. Potipher's wife got really mad. She lied to her husband and told him that Joseph tried to hurt her. Potipher became mad and sent Joseph to jail. Joseph spent a long time in jail. God did not forget Joseph.

Pharaoh had a dream and Joseph told Pharaoh what the dreams meant. They had to save food before the famine. Pharaoh made Joseph a ruler in Egypt.

Joseph was able to see his father Jacob again, and save his family from the famine. God had a plan for Joseph to care for his family.

Noah Builds the Ark

Noah and his family loved God.

God asked Noah to build an ark and fill it with animals.

42

It rained and rained and rained. It rained for 40 days and 40 nights. Water covered the whole earth.

Only Noah's family and the animals on the ark lived.

God put a rainbow in the sky as a promise that he would never flood the earth again.

Jonah and the Big Fish

The people living in the city of Nineveh were doing bad things. God had a message for them. God said to Jonah, "Go to Nineveh and let them know that I know what they are doing." Jonah did not like those people and he did not want to go. Instead, he tried to run away and hide from God.

Jonah got on a boat to sail far away. God threw a great wind onto the sea. Soon, a bad storm came and the ship started to sink. Jonah knew this was his fault for running away from God. The ship in which Jonah was travelling was in danger.

Jonah told the sailors to throw him overboard and the storm would stop. Jonah was thrown into the water and started to drown.

Even though Jonah was trying to hide from God, God knew exactly where he was. God loved Jonah and sent a big fish to rescue him. The fish opened its mouth and . . .

Swallowed Jonah! Jonah spent three days in the belly of the big fish. It was stinky and gross, but Jonah had time to think, pray, and ask God to forgive him.

God forgave Jonah and told the big fish to spit Jonah out on dry land. This time, when God told Jonah to go to Nineveh, he obeyed!

Jonah went to Nineveh with the message that God gave him. He told all the people about God's love.

The people listened to Jonah and asked God to forgive them. Because Jonah obeyed, they heard God's message and became followers of God.

David and Goliath

David lived in Bethlehem. He was the youngest son of Jesse, his father. David's job was to look after the family's sheep. He was a shepherd boy.

The Philistines always fought God's people. Their hero's name was Goliath. Goliath was a big, scary, mean giant. Every day, Goliath made fun of God and challenged God's people to fight him. But, everyone was too afraid to try.

David told the king that he would fight Goliath. He knew that God would help him.

46

David was too small to wear the heavy armor the king offered him. Instead, David chose five smooth stones and took his sling to go fight Goliath. Goliath laughed at him, but David wasn't scared.

David told Goliath that God would win this battle. David put a stone in his sling, swung it around and around, then let it go. It hit Goliath in the head and killed him. God saved his people once again!

That day, David won a great victory for Israel.

Job

A man named Job lived near Canaan. He was very rich, and also very good. Job and his wife had 7 sons and 3 daughters. Job also owned many animals; sheep, camels, cows, donkeys, and several people worked for him.

Satan felt that Job's life was easy and that was the only reason he was faithful to God. God told Satan he could test Job as long as he didn't kill him.

A servant came to Job and told him that most of his other servants and all of his animals had been killed. Then another servant came to him to tell Job that all of his children had been killed by a great wind. The wind had caused the house they were all in to collapse.

To all of this news, Job tore off his robe. He fell to the ground and said, "The Lord gave and the Lord has taken away; may the name of the Lord be praised."

Satan said that if Job became ill, he would surely be angry with God. So, Satan struck Job with skin sores causing him a great pain.

Job's wife was angry as she lost all of her children and possessions too. Job tells her he will not give up.

Job's friends – Eliphaz, Bildad, and Zophar – came to comfort him. They were concerned that Job must have done something wrong because it appeared God was punishing him.

However, this was not the case.

The Lord spoke to Job. Because he never turned away from God during his suffering, he was given back his health and belongings. Job was reminded that the Lord could do anything.

True or False

Which of these statements are true and which are false?
Write a "T" for true and an "F" for false.

| Jonah was swallowed by a whale. |  |  |

| Jesus was born in Egypt. |  |  |

| Daniel ate the king's food. |  |  |

| David killed Goliath with a slingshot. |  |  |

Birth of Jesus

Find the words listed below.

BETHLEHEM JOSEPH   WISE MEN
DONKEY   MANGER   ANGEL
HAY   MARY   SHEPHERD
JESUS   STAR

```
H J H M J Q R Y M H
A M O R S V G E D V
Y A H S N T H J D W
W N D R E E A R K I
L G M O L P E R L S
W E F H N H H E U E
W R T Y P K G S L M
V E R E V N E R G E
B A H N A J M Y K N
M S R N G X K T Q P
```

The Easter Story Domino Difference

The symbols on each domino match the domino next to it except for three. Circle the pieces that don't match.

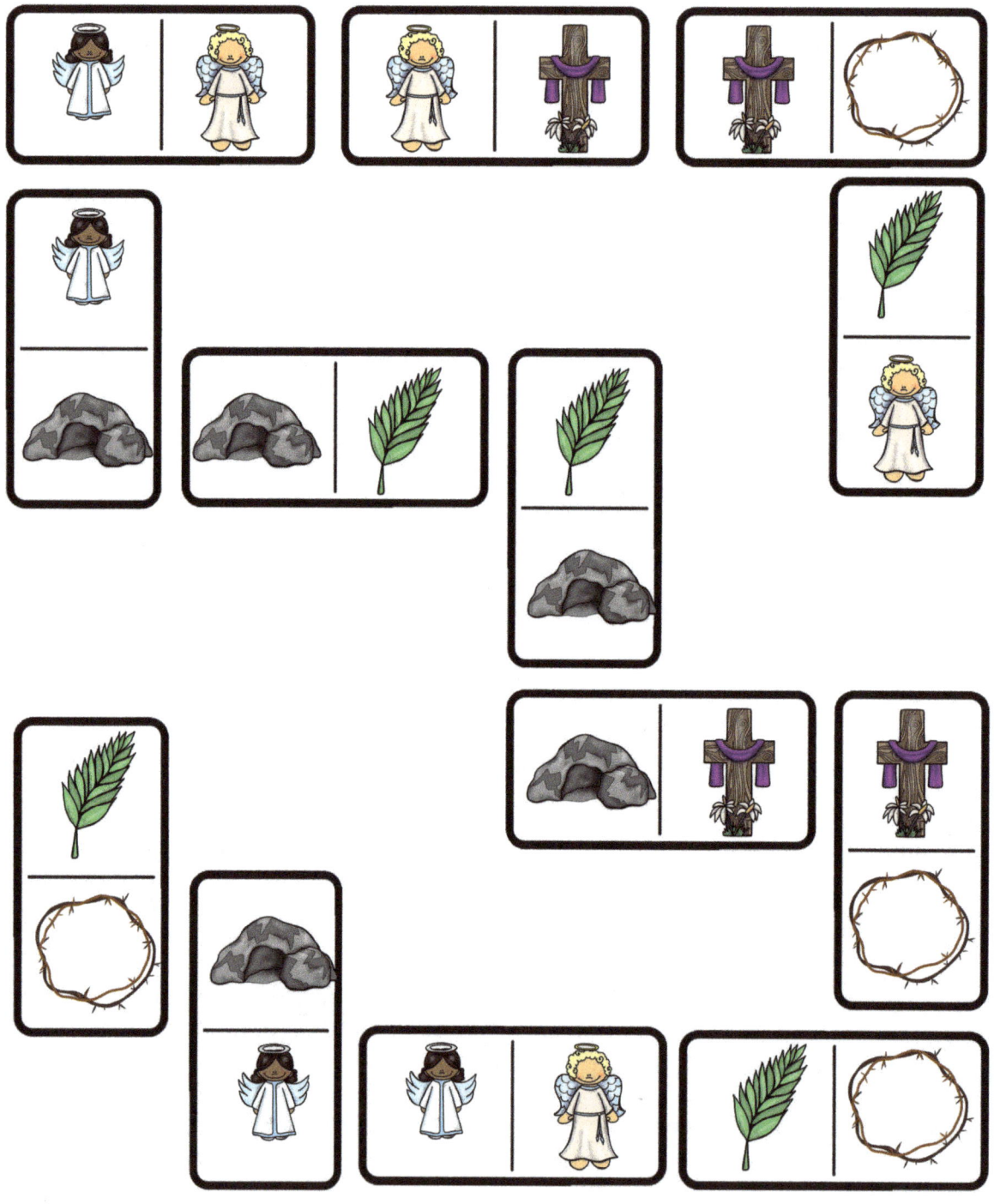

52

Plenty of Fish

Count how many fish there are and write your answer in the box below.

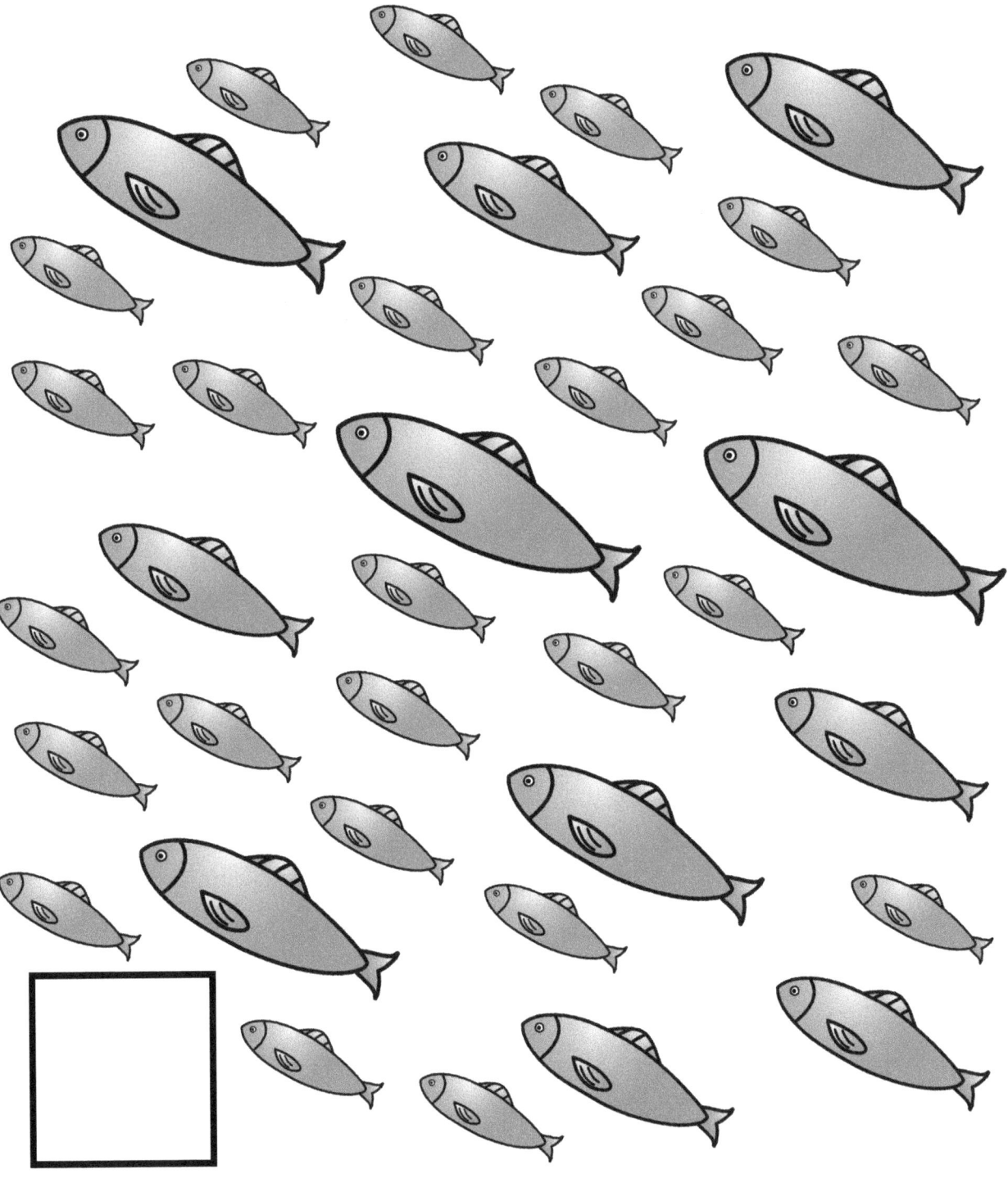

Answers

Birth of Jesus

Plenty of Fish

35 Fish

True or False

Jonah was swallowed by a whale. **T**
Jesus was born in Egypt. **F**
Daniel ate the king's food. **F**
David killed Goliath with a slingshot. **T**

Domino Match

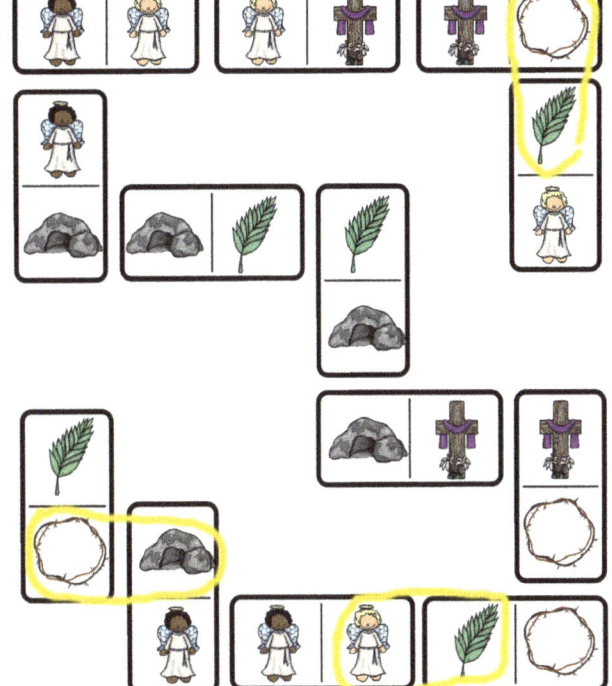

What Makes Me Special

Acceptance
I include others in play and conversation.

> **Verse to Memorize**
> Accept one another, just as Christ accepted you, in order to bring praise to God.
> Romans 15:7 NIV

Caring
I help others when they need it.

> **Verse to Memorize**
> None of you should look out just for your own good. Each of you should also look out for the good of others.
> Philippians 2:4 NIV

Cooperation
I work well with others to reach a common goal.

> **Verse to Memorize**
> Two people are better than one. They can help each other in everything they do.
> Ecclesiastes 4:9 NIV

Courage
I will overcome fear and stand up for what is right.

> **Verse to Memorize**
> I can do all things through Christ who gives me strength.
> Philippians 4:13 NIV

Forgiveness
I forgive others and ask others to forgive me.

> **Verse to Memorize**
> Forgive as the Lord forgave you.
> Colossians 3:13 NIV

Friendship
I am a good friend to others.

> **Verse to Memorize**
> A friend loves at all times. They are there to help when trouble comes.
> Proverbs 17:17 NIRV

Gentle and Kind
I say and do kind things for others.
I treat others with compassion.

> **Verse to Memorize**
> Let your gentleness
> be evident to all.
> The Lord is near.
> Philippians 4:5 NIV

Honesty
I will be truthful
in what I say and do.

> **Verse to Memorize**
> God, create a pure heart
> in me. Give me a new spirit
> that is faithful to you.
> Psalm 51:10 NIRV

Obedience
I obey God, my parents, my
teachers and authority.

> **Verse to Memorize**
> If you love me,
> obey my commands.
> John 14:15 NIRV

Patience
I wait calmly and nicely.

> **Verse to Memorize**
> When you hope, be joyful. When you suffer, be patient. When you pray, be faithful.
> Romans 12:12 NIRV

Peacemaker
I help stop others from fussing.

> **Verse to Memorize**
> So let us do all we can to live in peace. And let us work hard to build up one another.
> Romans 14:19 NIRV

Self-Control
I think before I speak and act.

> **Verse to Memorize**
> For the spirit God gave us does not make us timid, but gives us power, love and self-discipline.
> 2 Timothy 1:7 NIV

Thankful
I thank God for my food, family, friends, teachers, and my school.

Verse to Memorize
Give thanks to the Lord, for He is good. His love endures forever.
Psalm 136:1 NIV

Respect & Responsible
I treat others the way I want to be treated.
I do what I am supposed to do.
I take care of my books and copybook.

Verse to Memorize
Whatever you do, work at it with all your heart, as working for the Lord, not for human masters.
Colossians 3:23 NIV

www.ingramcontent.com/pod-product-compliance
Lightning Source LLC
Chambersburg PA
CBHW051400110526
44592CB00023B/2895